Rock Riffs

FOR UKULELE WITH TAB

ISBN 978-1-4803-9094-2

HAL•LEONARD® CORPORATION

7777 W. BLUEMOUND RD. P.O. BOX 13819 MILWAUKEE, WI 53213

Visit Hal Leonard Online at
www.halleonard.com

UKULELE NOTATION LEGEND

THE MUSICAL STAFF shows pitches and rhythms and is divided by bar lines into measures. Pitches are named after the first seven letters of the alphabet.

TABLATURE graphically represents the ukulele fingerboard. Each horizontal line represents a a string, and each number represents a fret.

Notes:

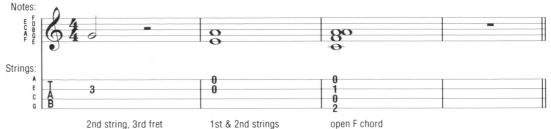

Strings:

2nd string, 3rd fret | 1st & 2nd strings open, played together | open F chord

---

HALF-STEP BEND: Strike the note and bend up 1/2 step.

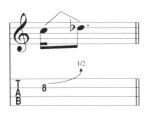

WHOLE-STEP BEND: Strike the note and bend up one step.

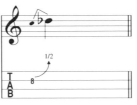

GRACE NOTE BEND: Strike the note and immediately bend up as indicated.

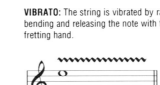

SLIGHT (MICROTONE) BEND: Strike the note and bend up 1/4 step.

BEND AND RELEASE: Strike the note and bend up as indicated, then release back to the original note. Only the first note is struck.

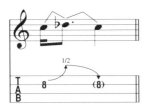

PRE-BEND: Bend the note as indicated, then strike it.

VIBRATO: The string is vibrated by rapidly bending and releasing the note with the fretting hand.

HAMMER-ON: Strike the first (lower) note with one finger, then sound the higher note (on the same string) with another finger by fretting it without picking.

PULL-OFF: Place both fingers on the notes to be sounded. Strike the first note and without picking, pull the finger off to sound the second (lower) note.

LEGATO SLIDE: Strike the first note and then slide the same fret-hand finger up or down to the second note. The second note is not struck.

SHIFT SLIDE: Same as legato slide, except the second note is struck.

TRILL: Very rapidly alternate between the notes indicated by continuously hammering on and pulling off.

TREMOLO PICKING: The note is picked as rapidly and continuously as possible.

Additional Musical Definitions

(accent)	• Accentuate note (play it louder)
(staccato)	• Play the note short
D.S. al Coda	• Go back to the sign (𝄋), then play until the measure marked "***To Coda***," then skip to the section labelled "**Coda**."
D.C. al Fine	• Go back to the beginning of the song and play until the measure marked "***Fine***" (end).
N.C.	• No chord.
	• Repeat measures between signs.
1. 2.	• When a repeated section has different endings, play the first ending only the first time and the second ending only the second time.

NOTE: Tablature numbers in parentheses mean:

1. The note is being sustained over a system (note in standard notation is tied), or

2. The note is sustained, but a new articulation (such as a hammer-on, pull-off, slide or vibrato) begins, or

3. The note is a barely audible "ghost" note (note in standard notation is also in parentheses).

from Free - *Fire and Water*

All Right Now

Words and Music by Andy Fraser and Paul Rodgers

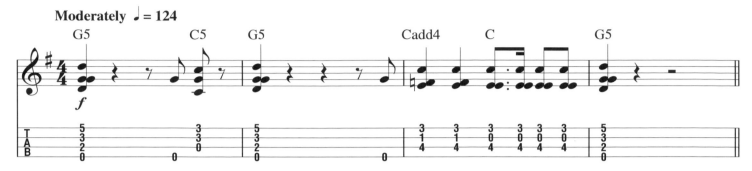

from Van Morrison - *Blowin' Your Mind*

Brown Eyed Girl

Words and Music by Van Morrison

from Coldplay - *A Rush of Blood to the Head*

Clocks

Words and Music by Guy Berryman, Jon Buckland, Will Champion and Chris Martin

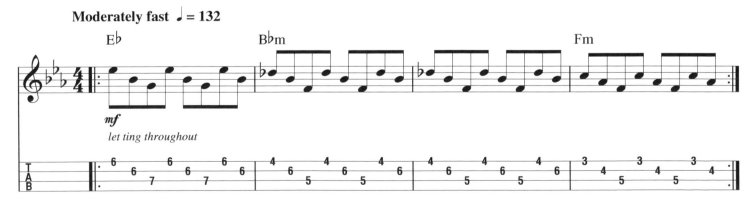

from AC/DC - *Back in Black*

Back in Black

Words and Music by Angus Young, Malcolm Young and Brian Johnson

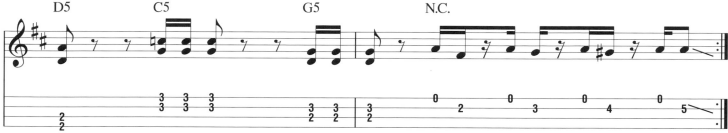

from Los Lonely Boys - *Los Lonely Boys*

Heaven

Words and Music by Henry Garza, Joey Garza and Ringo Garza

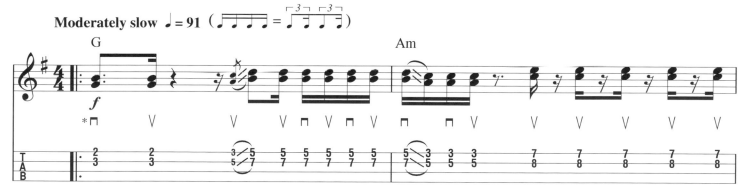

from Billy Idol - *Don't Stop*

Dancing with Myself

Words and Music by Billy Idol and Tony James

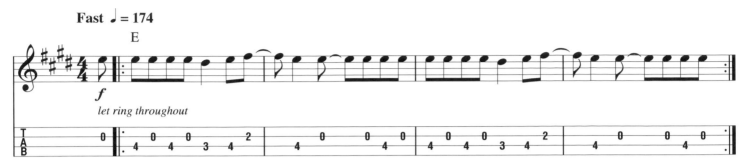

from Tommy Tutone - *Tommy Tutone-2*

867-5309/Jenny

Words and Music by Alex Call and James Keller

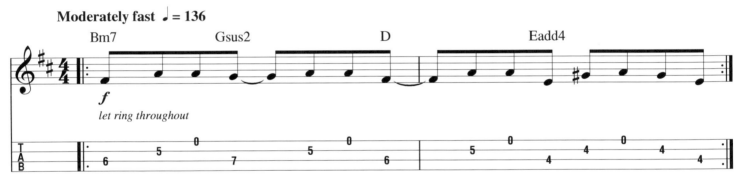

from Tom Petty - *Full Moon Fever*

Free Fallin'

Words and Music by Tom Petty and Jeff Lynne

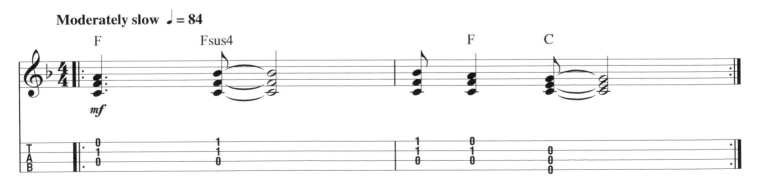

from The Mighty Mighty Bosstones - *Let's Face It*

The Impression That I Get

Words and Music by Dicky Barrett and Joe Gittleman

Very fast ♩ = 180

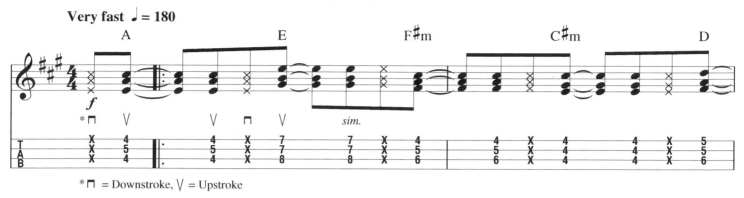

*⊓ = Downstroke, ∨ = Upstroke

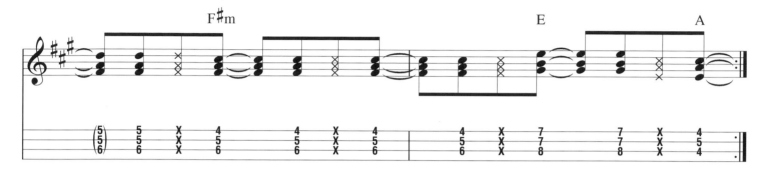

from The Doobie Brothers - *The Captain and Me*

Long Train Runnin'

Words and Music by Tom Johnston

Moderately ♩ = 116

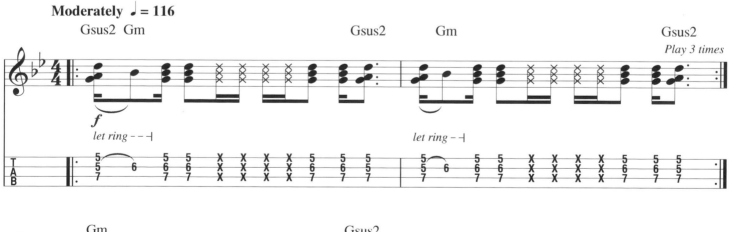

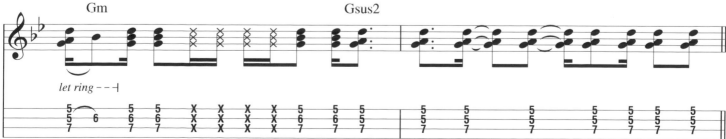

In My Life

Words and Music by John Lennon and Paul McCartney

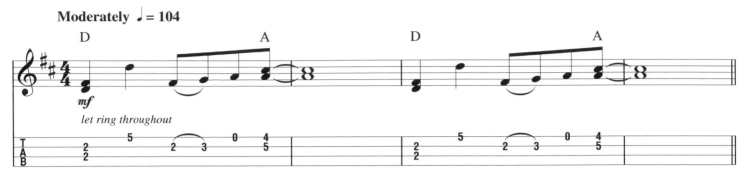

Iris

**from the Motion Picture CITY OF ANGELS
Words and Music by John Rzeznik**

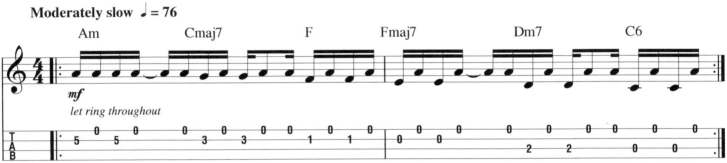

Louie, Louie

Words and Music by Richard Berry

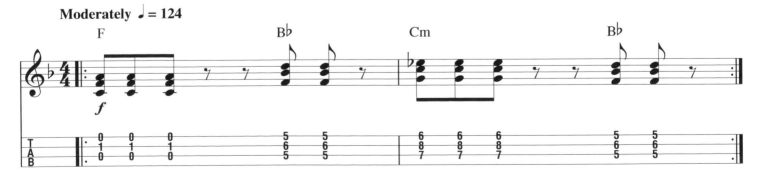

from Nirvana - *Unplugged in New York*

The Man Who Sold the World

Words and Music by David Bowie

from Foo Fighters - *The Colour and the Shape*

Monkey Wrench

Words and Music by David Grohl, Nate Mendel and Pat Smear

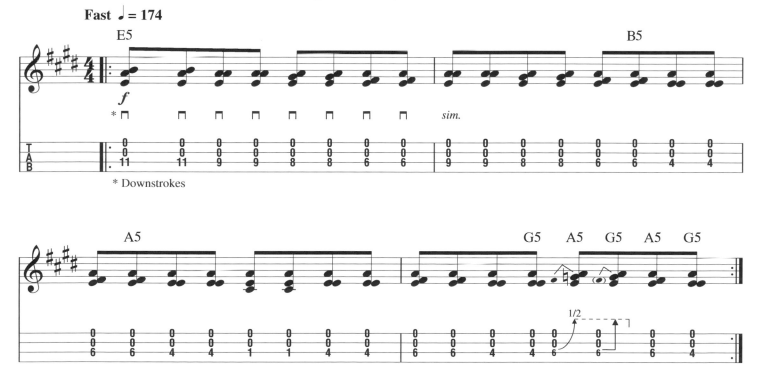

* Downstrokes

from Roy Orbison - *Orbisongs*

Oh, Pretty Woman

Words and Music by Roy Orbison and Bill Dees

* Downstrokes

from Weezer - *Weezer*

Say It Ain't So

Words and Music by Rivers Cuomo

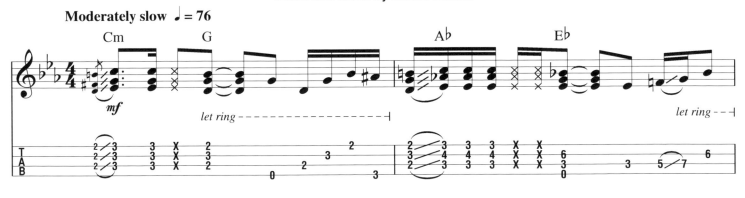

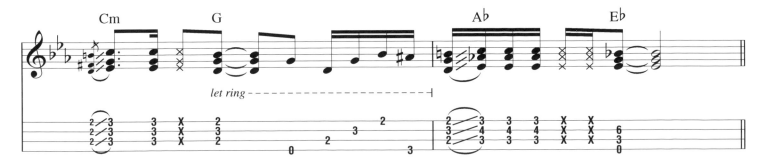

from Stone Temple Pilots - *Core*

Plush

Words and Music by Scott Weiland, Dean DeLeo, Robert DeLeo and Eric Kretz

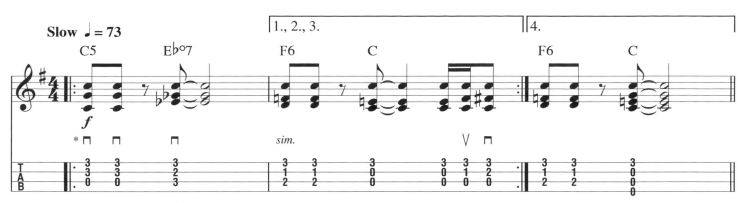

*□ = Downstroke, V = Upstroke

from David Bowie - *Diamond Dogs*

Rebel, Rebel

Words and Music by David Bowie

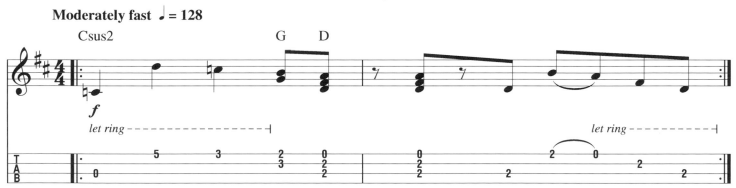

from Bob Seger & The Silver Bullet Band - *Nine Tonight*

Rock and Roll Never Forgets

Words and Music by Bob Seger

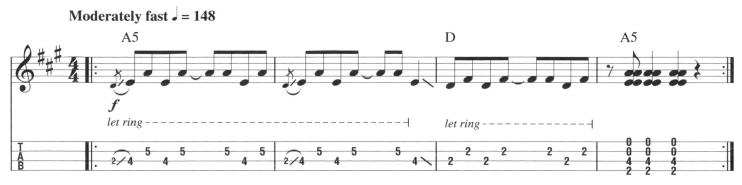

from Johnny Rivers - *And I Know You Wanna Dance*

Secret Agent Man

from the Television Series
Words and Music by P.F. Sloan and Steve Barri

from Queensrÿche - *Empire*

Silent Lucidity

Words and Music by Chris DeGarmo

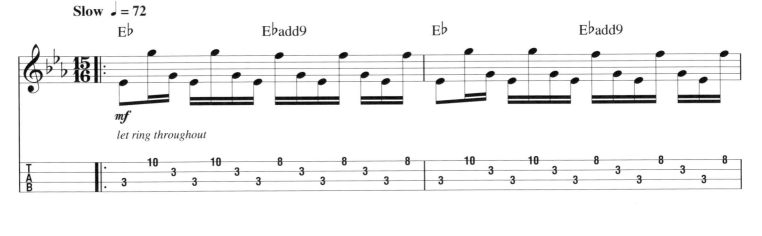

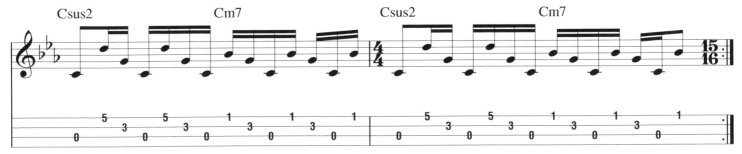

Smoke on the Water

Words and Music by Ritchie Blackmore, Ian Gillan, Roger Glover, Jon Lord and Ian Paice

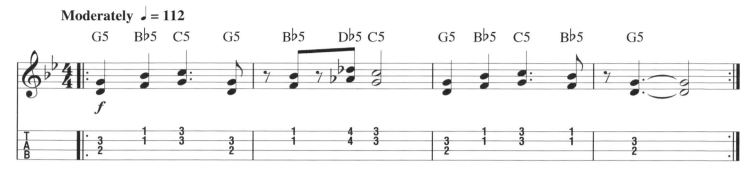

Spirit of Radio

Words and Music by Geddy Lee, Alex Lifeson and Neil Peart

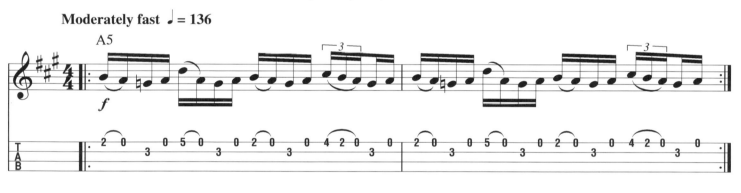

Ticket to Ride

Words and Music by John Lennon and Paul McCartney

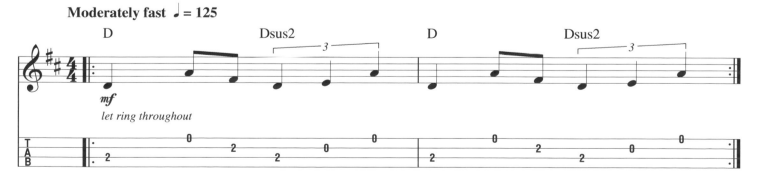

from U2 - *War*

Sunday Bloody Sunday

Words and Music by U2

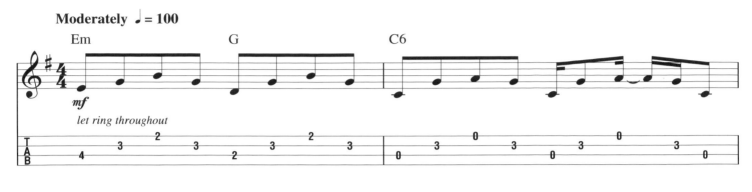

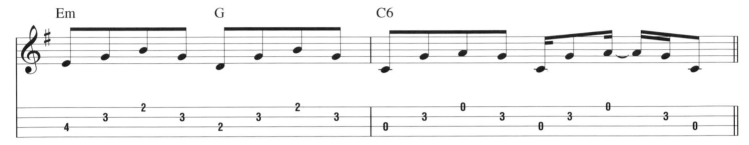

from Guns N' Roses - *Appetite for Destruction*

Sweet Child o' Mine

Words and Music by W. Axl Rose, Slash, Izzy Stradlin', Duff McKagan and Steven Adler

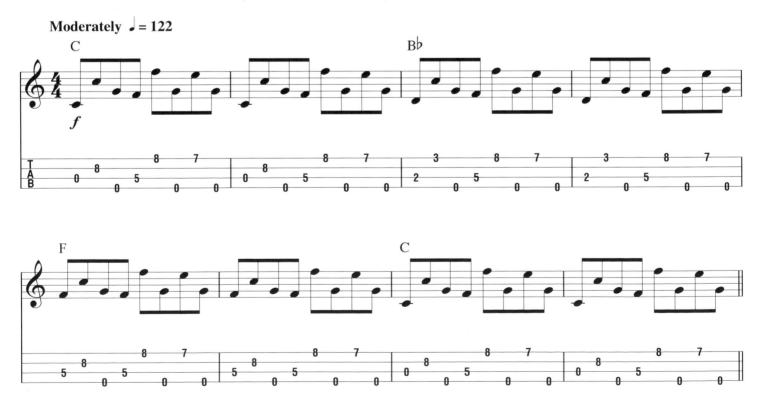

Up Around the Bend

Words and Music by John Fogerty

Wake Up Little Susie

Words and Music by Boudleaux Bryant and Felice Bryant

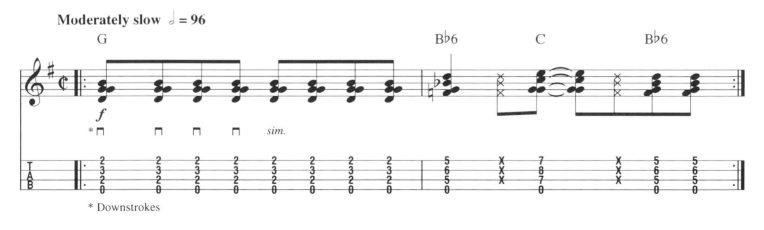

* Downstrokes

from AC/DC - *Back in Black*

You Shook Me All Night Long

Words and Music by Angus Young, Malcolm Young and Brian Johnson

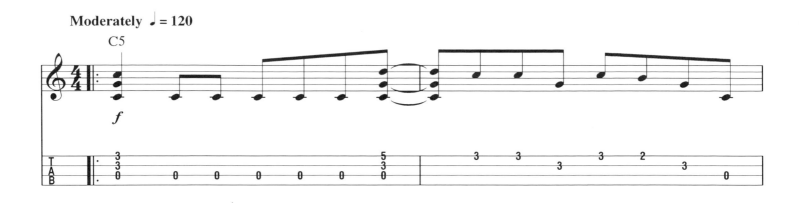

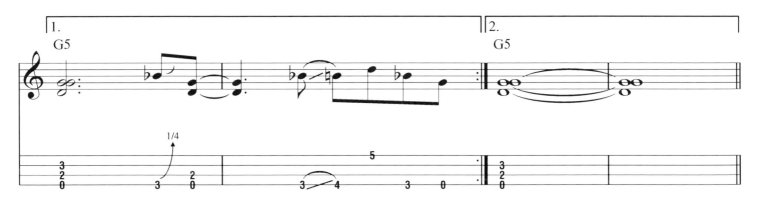